Cash Management Techniques

Roger W. Hill, Jr.

American Management Association, Inc.

190885

International standard book number: 0–8144–2146–6
Library of Congress catalog card number: 73–135670

Contents

1

Cash Management and Forecasting

Hɪsᴛᴏʀʏ is replete with examples of both good and bad cash management in private and public sectors of our economy. Periods of prosperity with their attendant speculative excesses have proved to be an outstanding burden to prudent cash management, and the failure to provide for adequate cash resources to meet liabilities as they come due has been one of the more common causes of business failures.

Although the concept of cash management is not new to the business world, important changes in the conduct of business since World War II have had a marked influence on its development. First, the expansion of corporations into the multidivisional or "profit center" structures stretching around the world has multiplied problems of controlling and funding corporate operations. Improvement of communications and transportation has facilitated innovations for the faster movement and clearing of funds. Corporations faced with a continuing cost-price squeeze on profits continue to search even harder for additional cost savings.

Perhaps the most important fundamental change that has occurred in our economy since World War II is the Employment Act of 1946, which has had a significant impact on the availability and cost of money. The twin objectives of reduced unemployment and a high standard of living with a minimal amount of inflation have produced such a strong consumer and social demand for goods and services that business and government have been hard pressed to satisfy it, even while utilizing all available credit.

Exhibit 1 gives an indication of how the increased demands for credit have been reflected in the rising cost of money over the past 25 years. Formerly, increasing costs of money have generally reduced the demand for it when growth and speculation became excessive; however, in recent years, cost has been less significant than the availability of funds in controlling the demand for money—as evidenced by the credit restrictions of 1966 and by a latent interest in the use of credit controls in highly inflationary periods.

Without some basic change in the economic structure, corporate financial officers must learn to live with expensive and limited supplies of money in a highly stimulated economy. Under these conditions, the role of the financial officer is destined to be more important in determining corporate policy and direction. He will be responsible for seeking ways to make more effective use of the corporate cash resources in order to satisfy the heavy cash demands to support the growth of the corporation. Furthermore, he will continue to play a significant role in improving the

Exhibit 1

Path of Short-Term Interest Rates, 1945–1970

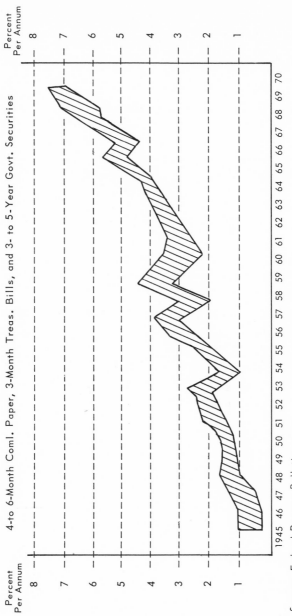

4-to 6-Month Coml. Paper, 3-Month Treas. Bills, and 3- to 5-Year Govt. Securities

Source: Federal Reserve Bulletin.

rate of return on corporate assets as underutilized cash is recycled into expanding operating assets or temporarily invested in the money market until it is needed to support corporate operations.

The Objectives of Cash Management

The main objective of cash management is a supportive one: to provide for the adequate availability and safekeeping of corporate funds under varied economic conditions in order to help achieve the desired corporate objectives.

Collecting receivables and paying bills have always been functions of cash management, but today cash utilization has taken on the additional perspective of evaluating the cost of money, or its ability to draw a return, in relation to the availability of required funds. Also, return on investment concepts are being applied more rigorously to such divisional or profit center assets as receivables, inventories, and plant and equipment, so that there is a trend toward increased utilization of cash throughout the corporation and increased cash availability at the corporate level under the supervision of the chief financial officer. Full utilization of monies under corporate management, therefore, focuses on their most economical use, their control and safekeeping, an assurance of adequate supply, and the temporary investment of excess funds. In order to achieve the first objective—the economical use of available cash—it is necessary to devise a plan to measure the funds required to run a corporation. Such a plan is a cash forecast.

Almost all corporations make use of some sort of cash forecast, although the forecasts will vary according to each corporation's approach to cash management, its cash position, and its attitude toward short-term investing. To the corporate financial officer intent on careful cash management, cash forecasts are a necessity; the effectiveness of his management will be greatly influenced by the accuracy and dependability of the forecast.

The Short-Term Forecast

Short-term forecasts can usually be made with great accuracy to serve many purposes, the first of which is to determine the cash requirements for financial operations. Once this amount has been established, management can determine whether it needs short-term financing and how much cash is available for temporary investments. Most short-term forecasts are designed to indicate the high and low points in a corporation's cash cycle, whether weekly, monthly, quarterly, or annually. Such an indication is particularly important to a company when the availability of money is critical, since it can preclude the necessity of borrowing by directing management to avoid scheduling large payments at times when the cash position will be low.

With a short-term forecast, the advantages of increasing inventories or receivables to accommodate sales can be measured against the cost and availability of the cash that will be required to finance such a buildup, and the financial officer will have adequate time to arrange for the necessary financing. If an inventory or receivable increase is unplanned, the financial officer will have a quick indication that something is wrong when the cash balance comes up short of his forecast. In periods of high cost and limited supplies of money, a lack of cash planning throughout an organization can be extremely costly and embarrassing.

A corporation with a large seasonal demand will find cash forecasts particularly helpful in estimating the amount of credit lines required from lending institutions, as well as the amounts of commercial paper that may be issued to aid in short-term financing. An accurate forecast will allow a corporation to minimize its cost of maintaining credit lines and borrowing. It may also indicate that cash is available for temporary investment, and can then assist in determining the portfolio mix of securities in terms of liquidity yield and maturity.

The length of the forecast. The time span covered in a short-term cash forecast will depend on the nature of the business in which the corporation is engaged. Generally, corporations whose operations are subject to wide fluctuations are more likely to use short forecasts, while more stable businesses will tend to employ longer forecasts. The purpose of a forecast will also influence its length. An aggressive investment program, for example, will require a forecast that is more detailed and of shorter duration than one prepared merely to provide a general idea of the projected cash balances for the year. Because every corporation has many different financial requirements, it is often necessary to prepare forecasts of varying periods for each particular purpose.

Forecasting methods. Two methods of short-term forecasting are commonly used: (1) the cash receipts and disbursements method and (2) the adjusted net income method. The cash receipts and disbursements method merely attempts to project the cash items received or disbursed, including operational and nonoperational items, items that arise from the projected purchase or sale of capital assets, and items that indicate increases or decreases in creditor or equity investment in the corporation.

The adjusted net income method (source and application of funds) projects changes in the balance sheet, particularly in working capital items. The estimated profit is adjusted for changes in working capital items that affect cash, such as receivables and inventory, and for nonoperating changes such as capital expenditures. A further adjustment is made for all noncash items such as depreciation expense.

Each method has certain advantages over the other for specific purposes. The cash receipts and disbursement method is more helpful in the day-to-day control of cash, while the adjusted net income method tends to produce a more accurate estimate of the cash position in forecasts for a quarter or longer. If both methods are used together, they can balance and supplement each other.

The Cash Receipts and Disbursements Method

Exhibit 2 shows a typical receipts and disbursements forecast. In such a forecast, estimates must be made for each source of cash as well as for each type of cash disbursement. The format shown here, of course, is only an example of the classifications that can be used; each corporation will have its own variations. The important consideration is to include those receipts and disbursements items that are important to the cash position of the individual corporation.

The sales, capital expenditure budgets, and production schedules provide the important data concerning the major recurring cash flows of the corporation. The corporate budget provides information concerning advances to subsidiaries, acquisitions, sales of assets, and other items that

Exhibit 2

Cash Receipts and Disbursements Method

	Last Year's Monthly Actual	This Year's Monthly Forecast	This Year's Monthly Actual	Increase or Decrease
Cash Receipts				
Collection on receivables by divisions				
Total collection on receivables				
Dividend income				
Sale of assets				
Other	_____	_____	_____	_____
Total cash receipts	=====	=====	=====	=====
Cash Disbursements				
Operating expenses by division				
Total operating expenses				
Income taxes				
Capital expenditures				
Payroll				
Advertising				
Insurance				
Repayment of debt				
Interest expense				
Dividends				
Other	_____	_____	_____	_____
Total cash disbursements	=====	=====	=====	=====
Excess cash disbursements	_____	_____	_____	_____
Excess receipts over disbursements	_____	_____	_____	_____
Cash and short-term investments Period beginning	_____	_____	_____	_____
Increase (decrease) in bank loans	_____	_____	_____	_____
Cash and short-term investments Period ending	_____	_____	_____	_____

have a nonrecurring effect on cash flows. Estimates for dividends and interest payments are relatively easy to develop, but such items as collections on receivables and raw material purchases require considerably more judgment when making projections. In addition to current estimates, actual results of prior years may assist the financial executive in evaluating the estimates used in making a forecast. A combination based on a compilation of actual results over prior years plus current corporate budgets gives the forecaster the basic tools that he needs.

Cash receipts and disbursements forecasts may be developed on a daily, weekly, or monthly basis. Daily and weekly forecasts are employed by corporations that must maintain tight control over cash or run an aggressive short-term investment program. Daily cash forecasts aid financial executives who want to have a clearer understanding of significant payment patterns and to be made immediately aware of any changes in payment trends that will affect the cash position. Monthly and quarterly forecasts are used to main a general control over the cash position.

The reliability of this forecast will rest heavily on the accuracy of the sales forecast. An error in sales estimates will generally show up as a corresponding error in the anticipated collections on receivables and will influence disbursements, because production schedules will be adjusted to changing sales.

On the receipts side of the forecast, collection on receivables is the most important projection. There are several ways of estimating collections. In some cases, collections will show a consistent tendency from actual past results to be a certain percentage of previous months' actual sales, depending on the terms given. In relatively stable businesses, the forecaster who performs a careful analysis of actual sales and the terms given can make very accurate short-run projections of cash receipts from receivables. In decentralized operations or those where collections fluctuate considerably, the forecaster must rely heavily on sales and credit managers, who have a better knowledge of current customer paying patterns.

On the disbursement side, the projection of operating expenses is also related to the sales forecast as seen in the production schedule. Estimates of operating expenses can be made on the basis of the payment terms of the corporate suppliers. Standard payments schedules, developed through the use of more extensive computer payments systems, can be of help in projecting dates for large disbursements. The most difficult problems encountered in short-term cash forecasting are caused by the dependence of the forecaster upon other people for basic data, and by the fact that the supplied information is often inaccurate—perhaps because the nature of the business makes forecasting unreliable or because the people supplying the information fail to do a careful job. Some other problems that arise in forecasting purchases are price changes on major items, vendors' failures to deliver on schedule, and forward buying necessitated by impending price increases, shortages, or strikes.

In forecasting capital expenditures, the division or area authorized to spend the funds must provide the data for estimates concerning the timing of actual payments. The major difficulty in accurately assessing the disbursements of funds for capital expenditures, particularly in new projects, arises from the difference between the scheduled progress of a project and the payment dates for construction actually completed.

Other items included in the forecast—such as taxes, payroll, advertising, and insurance—can best be determined from estimates given by the various departments involved. Also, if the financial officer is to forecast cash accurately, those responsible for large, nonrecurring items that affect cash must keep him constantly informed. No divisions or areas within the company should project anything affecting cash that falls outside their budgets unless they have made sure that it has been brought to the attention of the financial officer for use in his forecast.

Limitations of the method. The results of the completed cash forecast should provide a reasonably accurate estimate of the cash position and a good picture of all expected cash transactions. The method employed should be sufficiently flexible for short-range (daily and weekly) cash forecasting as well as for longer forecasts of a month's or three months' duration. But the forecast will have certain limitations. First, in daily projections of cash receipts, any disruption of normal business conditions caused by such problems as bad weather or strikes, which may delay the ordinary processing of cash items, will temporarily cause a variance between actual and projected cash receipts. However, as normal business conditions return, these distortions should be resolved in a reasonably short time.

A more significant limitation to the forecast is the fact that a receipts and disbursements approach cannot indicate the small, steady changes that may be taking place in the inventory or receivables balance. A subtle increase in inventory or receivables that does not stand out in the forecast may result in a substantial decrease in cash over a longer period of time, say, six months or a year. Because of this limitation, many financial officers supplement a cash receipts and disbursements forecast with another type of cash forecast that addresses itself to the problem of evaluating working capital accounts—the adjusted net income method.

The Adjusted Net Income Method

Exhibit 3 shows the format of a cash budget using the adjusted net income (funds) approach. This forecast is concerned with changes in balance sheet items, particularly working capital accounts. The sources of cash included in this forecast are net income, increases and decreases in working capital, depreciation and other noncash accounts, and nonoperating cash transactions.

Net income can be taken from the corporate profit budget. Nonoperating cash charges, such as dividends and debt installments due, are relatively easy to determine, as are such items as depreciation, provision for income taxes, and other noncash charges. Estimating the changes in working capital items, however, is the most important aspect of the forecast and the greatest challenge. The value of the forecast will be determined by the reliability of the estimates of receivables and inventories.

In relatively stable businesses, ratios can be developed on the basis of prior years' actual data for sales, receivables, and inventories. The financial officer may check the accuracy of these ratios by comparing actual receivables, inventory, and sales figures to insure that the ratios are still valid. If new trends are developing, the ratios must be adjusted accordingly.

When ratios based on past experience are not reliable, it is necessary to estimate changes in working capital accounts directly. Sales and credit managers can provide estimates of changes in receivables through their knowledge, their experience, and the current sales projection. The production department can also provide estimates concerning inventory levels for the period of the forecast. The greatest difficulty in accurately estimating changes in accounts receivable and inventory stems from such factors

Exhibit 3

Adjusted Net Income Method

	Last Year's 1st Qtr. Actual	*This Year's 1st Qtr. Forecast*	*This Year's 1st Qtr. Actual*	*Increase or De- crease*
Sources of Cash				
Net profit				
Income tax provision				
Depreciation				
Dividends paid by subsidiaries				
Sale of securities				
Other				
Total cash provided				
Uses of Cash				
Increase in accounts receivable				
Increase in inventories				
Increase in property, plant, and equipment				
Decrease in accounts payable				
Income tax paid				
Dividends paid				
Reduction in debt				
Other				
Total uses of cash				
Excess cash provided				
Cash and short-term securities Period beginning				
Increase (decrease) in bank loans				
Cash and short-term securities Period ending				

as lags in collection, changes in sales trends, and changes in the price of raw materials.

The divisions and profit-center areas provide capital expenditure estimates that include the projected cash disbursements for capital expenditures within the forecast period. These estimates, together with corporate requirements for cash in payment of dividends, income tax payments, and maturing debt, are included as a use of funds in the forecast.

The principal reason for employing the adjusted net income method is that it avoids the major weakness of the receipts and disbursements forecast by providing an accurate estimate of the cash position that takes into account the effect on cash by changes in working capital items. This is particularly important in divisionalized corporations where seasonal financial demands vary from one part of the corporation to another. The limitation of the adjusted net income approach is that it does not offer a day-to-day control over cash, since it does not trace the actual cash flow.

The strongest cash forecasting system generally combines the two methods, using a quarterly and annually adjusted net income forecast to check the adequacy of the credit lines and borrowing reserves, and a daily and monthly receipts and disbursements forecast to maintain close control over the cash position and aid in the full investment of temporary cash surplus.

Forecasting is not an exact science and cash forecasts will inevitably be at variance with the actual result. However, to increase the effectiveness of a cash forecast, a cash management system should have some procedure for comparing forecast figures with the actual results, when they are available, in order to analyze significant differences; such differences may indicate that important factors affecting cash were not used in the original assumptions.

A comparison with actual results may also provide a means for evaluating the forecasting procedures and indicate how improvements may be made in the future. Thus it serves as a means of stimulating interest and care on the part of those people involved in preparing and supplying information for the forecasts.

Cash projections may be revised monthly or quarterly to maintain a current forecast for periods varying from a month to a year ahead. Such revisions may be formal or informal, and are made by inserting the actual figures of the period just completed and adjusting the future periods without revising the entire forecast with new estimates. Any time significant changes occur that affect cash, informal revisions may be made to update and improve the accuracy of the forecast. Very short-range forecasts are usually revised only at the end of the forecast period.

The Long-Term Forecast

In contrast to the short-term cash forecast, which goes into detail, the long-term cash forecast attempts to show only significant changes caused by acquisitions, the introduction of new products, and the long-term growth of the corporation. Such a forecast should indicate whether sufficient cash will be generated to support the corporate operations in the future. It will also show when a corporation can expect to run out of money and the reasons why. Using this forecast, the financial officer is in a better position to determine how much money must be borrowed and how long it will take to repay the borrowed funds, whether the funds raised should be long-term or temporary borrowing, and what the effect will be on the capital structure. This in turn will help management determine what it can afford and what programs should be approved, deferred, or abandoned.

A comprehensive long-term forecast not only indicates to management its financial capabilities, but also assists in securing the funds necessary to finance corporate plans, since lenders are shown a comprehensive cash forecast indicating when funds are required and how repayment will be made.

The methods used in long-term forecasting are the same as those used in short-term forecasting, although the adjusted net income approach is preferred. The estimates used in long-term forecasts are less detailed and less accurate, because of the longer projections involved, and there is a greater dependence on forecasts prepared by other departments within the corporation. The purpose of a long-term forecast is to focus attention on long-term cash needs for operations and capital spending in relation to current corporate liquidity and capital structure.

2

Cash Control
and Safekeeping

Mᴏᴅᴇʀɴ cash management originally developed out of a custodial function—cash control and safekeeping—and although its role today has been expanded and has become more sophisticated, the safeguarding of funds still remains a key part of cash management.

The Importance of Centralization

The centralized management of cash is an important asset in safeguarding and controlling funds. Even while corporations are becoming divisionalized and decentralized on an operating basis, cash control has continued to be a function centralized under direct corporate management. The use of deposit accounts under central control, for example, permits local offices to make deposits, but allows only those responsible for cash control to transfer money out of the account. On the disbursement side, the use of an imprest account limits the size of the balance held in a bank account to the amount necessary to compensate for the services provided and to meet operating needs while safeguarding the funds. The use of such an account requires that receipted bills from the local office be presented to the centralized control before the account can be replenished.

Centralized control of signing and borrowing authority prevents the unauthorized expenditure of funds, as do the control of all bank signing and borrowing resolutions and the use of countersigning for borrowing and disbursing monies on behalf of the corporation. Additional precautions that are necessary when facsimile signatures are used include a fixed responsibility for adequate safekeeping of facsimile plates, a record of the number of times the plates are used and the number of checks that are issued and/or spoiled, and the manual signing of all large disbursements over a specified amount.

When the cash function is centralized, less cash is required to support normal corporate operations, since fewer banks are used and therefore the balances required to serve as a buffer against uncertainty and as compensation for services are smaller. This also avoids tying up funds in many local bank accounts when such funds would be more valuable if used in supporting major banking relationships.

A corporation that centralizes the control of cash is better able to generate a large enough volume of work to justify using specialists in cash analysis and short-term investing. It also strengthens control by fixing the responsibility for standard methods and procedures throughout the corporation and placing the operation of bank accounts in one central authority.

In a decentralized organization, there must be an unusually strong plan for providing the financial officer with the information necessary to manage the cash position and control the authorized use of divisional bank accounts. All locations must submit forecasts of the cash that is to be received or disbursed from their bank accounts, so that the total amount of money available within the organization can be determined and decisions can be made on borrowing requirements, intradivisional flow of funds, capital expenditures, and the temporary investment of excess cash. If reliable cash forecasts are not forthcoming, effective central control of cash will be severely undermined, and there will have to be more direct centralized control of field operations concerning the use of money.

Collection of Receivables

The reduction of the time necessary for collecting receivables is an area of cash management that is completely under the purview of the financial officer and has great potential for providing additional usable cash. This can be done by one of two banking arrangements, area concentration banking or a lockbox system. The objective of either approach is to reduce the mail delivery time required to receive a check for processing and also to reduce the time required to convert the payment to "collected" funds that are available for use by the corporation. For example, if deposits average $100,000 a day and the mailing and collecting time can be reduced by three days, this is the equivalent of "finding" $300,000 of usable funds. With the cost of money at 8 percent, the value of those found funds would be $24,000 a year—a sizable saving!

Area concentration banking. Concentration systems are

most useful in improving the collections of corporations with a large number of field offices throughout the country that collect a large volume of small payments. The flow of funds is illustrated in Exhibit 4.

A special grouping of banks and bank accounts with certain characteristics will help achieve this freeing of funds. Banks serving as central collecting locations should be in Federal Reserve cities and should be on the bank wire system; banks used as depositories should receive approximately 80 to 90 percent of the checks one day after they are mailed by the customer. Bank charges and fees should be competitive.

The area concentration system provides that local offices receive and deposit checks in banks in their local areas. The funds are moved from the local banks to regional or area banks by bank wire (if bank wire is available and if the amount warrants the expense) or transfer check. Compensating balances to cover the cost of service or to protect credit lines are usually maintained at the regional or area banks. Local banks may be compensated by balances or by a fee negotiated between the bank and the corporation.

The daily reports of collected funds received by the corporation's major bank from the regional banks are reported to the financial officer, who can draw off excess funds from the system and have such money available for investment or disbursement as needed. As an alternative, collected funds over a specified amount can be transferred automatically to the corporation's main bank, but this limits the flexibility involved in drawing down cash from the regional accounts to meet seasonal requirements, allowing the balances to build up in slack periods, and using an annual average compensating balance.

The lockbox system. The second method for speeding up collections is a lockbox system. This is a system of de-

Exhibit 4
Area Concentration Banking

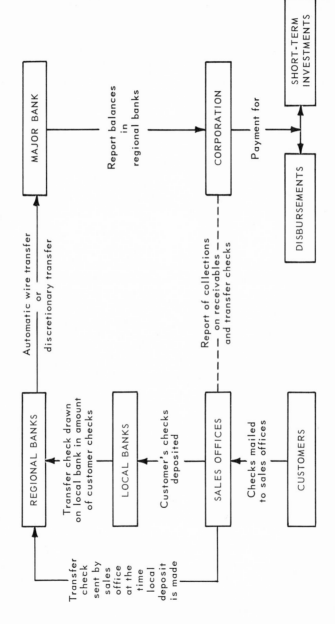

pository accounts geographically located so that payments mailed by customers will take no more than one day to reach that location. The flow of funds is illustrated in Exhibit 5. The lockbox is a post office box designated as the remittance address for customers of the corporation. The corporation then authorizes its bank to have access to this post office box, allowing the bank to collect mail from the post office several times a day, process the checks, and forward the details received with the checks to the corporation's credit and accounts receivable departments for posting. In this way, receivables checks can be processed before the accounting function takes place rather than some time afterward.

The lockbox is of value primarily to corporations whose accounts receivable are centralized and in which there is a sufficient number of checks of large dollar amounts to warrant the cost of processing. The advantage of the lockbox system is that collected funds are available at least one to three days sooner than under ordinary corporate processing where checks are sent to the corporate headquarters.

The lockbox system has encountered certain difficulties as a result of its own efficiency. Some customers may resent the sudden speed with which their remittances are processed and cleared through their banks—with a resulting drop in the funds available to them—and they may adopt remittance policies to compensate for the faster collection of checks. Credit managers may find the policing of credits more difficult, since they receive the details pertaining to deposits a day or two later than normal, unless a wire system to transmit the credit and collection details is employed. The lockbox also precludes the holding of a customer's check by the credit department so that it may be deposited on a later date by mutual agreement between a customer and the credit manager.

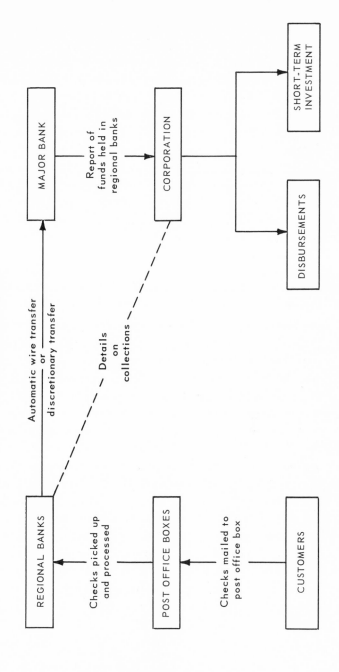

Exhibit 5

The Lockbox System

Because both methods described here have their advantages and limitations, most corporations will probably develop a system that combines the two and, in addition, allows for deposits made by corporate headquarters under special circumstances. Any system for improving the processing and collection of checks can be assisted by effective credit procedures. The credit organization may be decentralized to assist a particular division in giving better service to customers and having closer contact with slow-paying customers. Or a corporation may help a customer establish better financial and management control, which in turn will strengthen the customer's ability to pay more promptly.

Invoicing Procedures

One way to improve the availability of cash is to avoid delays in invoicing. A system that can handle seasonal peak loads quickly and accurately can materially aid in eliminating the costly delays and lost collection time that result from mailing out invoices several days after shipments have been made. An additional improvement can be made if a successful invoicing system enables a corporation to have customers pay on individual invoices rather than on the basis of monthly statements.

If invoicing is under centralized control and shipments are made from warehouses throughout the country, the use of computer terminals and teletype systems can save significant amounts of time in sending information concerning shipments, invoicing, and inventory levels from the plants and warehouses to the corporate headquarters.

Errors in invoicing may prove even more expensive than delays, since many corporations will not make payment until they receive a corrected invoice. Poor billing procedures result in the delayed receipt of cash just as a poor receivables collection system does. The lost time in both cases means less available cash to gain a return or reduce borrowing requirements.

Payables Systems

Cash can be conserved by employing a sound payables system that centralizes the payment of large bills as far as it is practicable to do so. This allows for the careful timing of disbursements, the ability to take offered discounts, and the possible use of drafts rather than checks.

A centralized payables system facilitates control over the timing of disbursements and the reduction of funds required in divisional accounts. By carefully matching expected collections and disbursements, the corporation can avoid fluctuating between sudden cash drains, which may force it to borrow funds for very short periods, and unusually large cash buildups.

Discounts should always be taken when offered, and they should be processed in such a way that they are paid as late in the discount period as possible, but always before the discount expires. A policy of mailing payments late in the day or on Fridays is an additional method employed occasionally to gain additional mail time for conserving cash.

Drafts constitute a technical device that can give a financial officer added flexibility. A draft differs from a check in that it is not held to be a claim against corporate funds until it is presented to the appropriate bank for payment. Once the draft is presented, the corporation may or may not honor it; if it does, it may take one business day to raise the funds. When checks are issued, the corporation has, in effect, made payment when the vendor receives them, and funds must be available when the checks clear. Of course, if a corporation expects vendors to accept its drafts as payment, it must always honor them.

The main reason for the use of drafts is to maintain stricter control over the collected balance in the bank account without violating laws concerning the issuance of checks in amounts exceeding the funds in a bank account. It allows a corporation to run negative cash balances in the corporate cash books in order to reduce the high balances that may be reported on a bank statement because of a large number of outstanding checks.

The original purpose of the payable-through-draft was to give a corporation with decentralized operations a system for allowing divisions to draw against the major bank accounts while under central control, with the financial officer having the right to refuse to honor the draft if the expenditure had not been approved. It is true, however, that some vendors complain that a company's use of drafts may create collection problems for them, since they must be put in for collection rather than being deposited as a routine matter.

Inventory Control

Although inventory can tie up considerable amounts of cash, inventory control does not normally come under the direct control of the financial officer, as do the activities relating to the freeing of collected funds from receivables. For a perspective on inventory and cash requirements, standards may be developed either from inventory ratios (the relationship of inventory to sales) or from records of the corporation's past experiences. When it appears that the inventory investment is beginning to run high and consume increasing amounts of cash, the financial officer can bring this to the attention of corporate management and the division or area. Steps can then be taken to reduce the inventory buildup or, if necessary, to make plans for raising cash to accommodate the increase.

The Use of Fixed Assets

Other means to conserve cash involve large capital expenditures and the use of fixed assets. There are tax options, for example, that permit a corporation to continue to use cash that ordinarily would not be available until a later time. Savings can be gained when the cash flow of an asset is increased by the use of accelerated depreciation and taxes are postponed. A postponement of taxes also results when construction costs and research are expensed currently rather than being capitalized.

The practice of leasing, in which a corporation pays for an asset while using it, gives the corporation the use of assets without the necessity of tying up valuable cash over a long period of time in outright purchase. Corporations in fast-growing, profitable businesses with limited capital find leasing an extremely favorable method for obtaining the use of an asset that they could not otherwise afford. The sale and leaseback of existing facilities may be a source of cash for a corporation as well.

3

Corporate-Bank Relations

Bₐₙₖ relations are important to the corporation; it is through the banking system that a financial executive implements his cash management plan, and the careful selection and use of deposit, imprest, and regular bank accounts contribute to the most efficient control and safekeeping of cash. The lending capacity of the banking system further provides a corporation with flexibility in financing seasonal requirements and special transactions. Although the extent and complexity of a corporate-bank relationship may vary with the number of banks and services required, no cash management program can be complete without an effective one.

Selection of Banks

The tools that can assist the financial executive in managing the banking function have been discussed earlier, in connection with cash forecasting, control, and safekeeping. However, before the financial executive considers the banks that his corporation may use, he must identify its cash requirements. Daily, weekly, and monthly cash forecasts will give a good indication of the receipts and disbursements that can be expected and will help determine what operating cash balances are required. Once these balances are established, future requirements can be determined from the long-range forecast. This gives the financial officer the necessary information for planning his bank selection.

The prime consideration for the corporate financial officer is to develop an adequate alignment of banking facilities to handle present and future financial requirements. He must analyze the ability of a bank to transfer funds, handle deposits, accommodate operating accounts—including imprest, lockbox, and payroll accounts—assist in overseas transactions, extend credit and financing, provide assistance in investing surplus cash, disburse dividends, extend custodial or trustee services, and be registrar or transfer agent for the corporate securities.

The number and distribution of accounts depends largely upon the size of the operating balances required, the geographical location of corporate facilities, and the amount of bank credit that may be required. Many smaller-size corporations can function very well with only one or two major banking relations, supplemented by a few accounts at banks near plant locations. In most instances there is good reason for concentrating bank accounts in a few banks; it enables a corporation to maximize its importance as a customer to a particular bank. The larger the account, the more incentive there is for the banker to be accommodating. Also, with several different operating accounts in one bank, the transfer of funds from one account to another is simplified and the corporation may treat all accounts as one in determining the profit or loss of the relationship to the bank. As a result, profitable accounts may be used to offset expenses of unprofitable accounts or some services provided by the bank on behalf of the corporation. Other factors that play an important role in the development of banking relations may be the corporation's role in the community, payroll facilities for employees, business relationships, and directorships.

The selection of a bank may also be influenced by the size of the bank. A financial officer of a smaller-size company may feel that he can receive better service from a smaller-size bank where he is a relatively larger depositor. However, the amount of credit that a bank may extend to a customer is limited by its size—specifically, its capital, surpluses, and undivided profits when allowed by law— and therefore some corporations may not wish to support a large number of small credit lines when a few lines from larger banks would be adequate.

The character of a bank may have a strong influence on a corporate financial officer's decision. A bank noted for its ability to handle foreign transactions will be sought by corporations heavily involved in overseas business; another noted for its lockbox planning and wire facilities will be sought by corporations with large receivables collection problems. A bank with aggressive management that is willing to provide additional services and accommodations at competitive costs will appeal to a corporate financial officer, while a bank that appears uninterested and charges high fees for services will get little consideration.

Because the financial condition of a bank is so important, the bank's financial strength should be reviewed periodically to be sure that the corporate funds on deposit are not endangered by poor bank management. It is true that the FDIC insures smaller balances, but it does not protect the bulk of any sizable deposit. More protection against bad management is afforded by a periodic examination under federal and state regulations. A corporate financial officer can keep himself informed of a bank's financial condition with a few simple ratios: a comparison of capital funds with liquid assets, with deposits, and with loans. Such tests should give an indication of the bank's operations and point out any changes in the character of the bank or its operations.

When a corporation has a thorough knowledge of the size and condition of the banking facility that it is using, it can avoid endangering corporate deposits that appear large in relation to the bank's capital. An interesting sidelight on this situation is that unusually large deposits in a particular bank may cause the bank to be criticized by its other customers as being controlled by a dominant corporate depositor.

Evaluation and Compensation

Most banking services are paid for by the interest-bearing cash balances in a corporation's accounts, which enable the bank to cover the costs of maintaining the relationship and to make a profit. The greatest difficulty involved in using compensating balances, both for the corporation and for the bank, is that of determining the value of the required banking services.

The banking system as a whole has made considerable progress in defining its costs and evaluating such items as deposits, paid checks, wire transfers, other operating services, and the earning power of balances. However, such progress has not led to any simple formula; different banks have different cost problems, different asset structures, different capitalization, and different regulatory requirements. There simply are no standard costs for banking services.

A corporation may attempt to analyze its accounts with various banks by asking each bank to evaluate its account and indicate what service charges will be required to operate the account satisfactorily, as well as what earning value it will assign to the corporate balance to offset charges. If the corporation does this for all its accounts, the chances are that no two analyses will be alike, since some banks will assign higher charges and higher earnings than others. The advantage of having banks establish their costs and earnings on corporate accounts is that it enables the corporation to evaluate and compare costs and services and to set standards for other banks that may be considered.

A further refinement in analyzing the comparative costs of services is to group together banks of comparable size and location. A large city bank's operating costs and earnings on deposits will not be the same as those of a small rural bank, and the two should not be grouped together. Once the banks are categorized, the corporation can develop average cost standards and average earning rates on balances. These standards can then be applied to all account relationships and used to determine whether charges of a particular bank are out of line.

Bank Account Analysis

A simple format for the evaluation of various bank accounts is illustrated in Exhibit 6. It includes the total funds available to a bank for investment, the monthly rate of earnings, the charges for various services provided, and the difference between charges and earnings. Such a format will enable a corporate officer to be fair to all his accounts in relation to the services they provide.

Exhibit 6

Bank Account Analysis

Bank   _____
Accounts   _____
Month   _____

CASH AVAILABILITY
    Average daily book balance   _____
less: Average daily uncollected funds   _____
    Average daily collected funds
    balance   _____
less: Reserves required by Federal
    Reserve   _____
    Average daily balance available
    for bank investment   _____

STANDARD BANK EARNINGS RATE _____%
Value of funds available to the bank   _____

STANDARD COST OF SERVICES	NO. OF ITEMS	UNIT COST	TOTAL COST
Checks deposited			_____
Checks paid			_____
Wire transfer			_____
Account maintenance			_____

Cost of services provided by the bank   _____

Net value over cost   _____

This kind of analysis, however, does not take into consideration such important matters as credit lines and the lending capacity of the bank. Although the operational services provided by a bank do assist in the control and safekeeping of corporate funds, the availability of credit in the future is vital to corporate cash planning and must also be provided for. Part of the compensating balance technique of paying for banking services provides for compensation in return for an agreement to supply a certain amount of credit if the need should arise. Historically, the guide used has been an expected balance of approximately 10 percent of a line requested and 20 percent of the amount of the line used. This guide has at best been a very flexible one and in fact may serve only as a starting point in negotiating credit availability. Corporations that have not relied heavily on their lines may negotiate compensating balances somewhat below these figures, while undercapitalized corporations may be required to keep a higher amount.

There is no simple formula for establishing the correct levels of balances necessary to maintain good bank relations. Much depends upon the corporation's understanding of the problems of a bank in maintaining a profitable relationship, as well as the bank's understanding of what corporate services are required and its ability to supply these services adequately when they are needed. As long as compensating balances are used as a method of payment for banking services, negotiation between the corporate officer and the banker will probably be the means for determining the level of balances required; however, both sides appear to be assembling more reliable data to serve as the basis for their negotiations and provide more satisfactory results for both parties.

4

Cash Availability and Temporary Investing

THE biblical parable of the talents, describing the ultimate fate of the man who buried his talent in the ground, may be the first recorded failure of a short-term money manager. The primary objectives of short-term investment are twofold in the area of cash management: safety of principal (the creditworthiness of the investment and its marketability) and yield (return). The poor soul in the parable achieved one effectively but failed to achieve the other, and in determining policy concerning the investment of excess cash both objectives must be accommodated.

Development of Policy

The return of dollars on monies invested is a relatively simple concept until a question is raised about the different yields on various short-term instruments or the variations in yield on a given security over a period of time. The disparity of yields on different types of investments indicates the quality of the credit and its marketability; an increase in yield usually means some sacrifice in the safety and/or marketability of the investments.

Safety and marketability deal with the degree of certainty with which the principal can be recaptured on or before maturity without serious loss. Marketability can be affected most seriously by general economic and money conditions that may cause material loss of principal on even a high-quality credit instrument that must be sold before maturity.

In the development of policy for the investment of surplus funds, the intended use of those funds is as important as the corporate return-on-investment philosophy concerning the use of short-term funds. If the invested funds are to be used as a return of cash into inventory and receivables as seasonal business develops, or as a cushion against a sudden unexpected drain of cash, a highly marketable, minimum principal risk investment will probably be considered. If the funds are intended for a specific payment at some time in the future, as a dividend or tax payment, a security maturing on that date may be purchased with less concern for marketability. Finally, if there are general excess funds over and above seasonal or specific purposes, they may be invested in securities with longer maturities or less marketability, provided that the increase in yield from these securities is adequate to make the risk worth while.

Corporate management's philosophy of investments will directly influence the risk taken and the yield received. If management takes the view that short-term investments are a profit center on a par with operating divisions, it may develop a high-risk, high-yield attitude; however, such an attitude can cause the solvency of the corporation to be more vulnerable under adverse economic conditions. On the other hand, a management with adequate reserves to protect bank relations may consider any return better than just leaving the funds idle. A yield compensated by assured corporate liquidity against more difficult times may be sufficient for many managements. Appendix 1 indicates the amount of interest earned per day at various interest levels per $1 million of investment.

A surplus cash position that continues to grow beyond the bounds of capital expenditures and seasonal and projected requirements may indicate the need to weigh a dividend payout against a continued investment of surplus reserves not committed to future corporate planning. The amount of funds available and the size and quality of the staff required to conduct day-to-day investment operations will influence a corporate investment policy. If the funds are of sufficient size to return relatively large sums, and if corporate management has confidence in the ability of the staff to invest prudently as economic conditions change, the policy will probably be broader and more flexible. In general, however, the actual return in after-tax dollars on a broad exposure of large sums of money for limited periods of time makes many corporate policies relatively conservative.

The appearance of a surplus cash position is generally not the result of a conscious effort on the part of management to create a new profit center in money market activities, but rather the result of overall corporate financial planning to assure future growth and corporate liquidity under various economic conditions.

Types of Investments

The following paragraphs describe some of the common money market instruments available for investment; a more detailed breakdown can be found in Appendix 2.

Treasury bills. Direct obligations outstanding form the largest group of available securities in the money market. Treasury bills provide the highest-quality market instrument for investment because of the government's ability to repay its obligations through taxation or new money printings. A Treasury bill may in fact be considered currency that yields a return to the holder.

Several major government dealers make a sizable market in Treasury bills, which are offered weekly on Monday for payment on Thursday with three-month and six-month maturities. There are also special issues of bills with maturities of up to one year that are sold toward the end of each month to supplement the weekly offerings and are used to assist in Treasury financing.

Bills are sold at a discount from their face value; the stated value is returned at maturity, and the difference represents the return to the investor. Unless there is a dramatic change in the national economy and level of interest rates, Treasury bills can be sold before maturity with little or no risk of principal loss because of the great demand for these securities in the money market. Appendix 3 indicates a method of measuring the decline in yield necessary to cause a principal loss.

A special offering of Treasury bills may be used in payment of income taxes. These "tax anticipation" issues mature about a week after the quarterly income tax dates. As a result, a corporation that uses such bills in payment of taxes receives about a week's free interest. The use of such bills, however, must be weighed against the advantages to

44

the bank-corporate relationship of corporate tax payments paid through a bank and credited to its tax and loan account—a one- to two-week availability of such funds to the bank may be allowed by the Treasury.

Other Treasury obligations, such as Treasury notes and bonds, although they do not have the same broad market acceptance as do Treasury bills, have the same high credit protection. Certain capital gains and refunding practices by the Treasury can make investment in bonds and notes that are approaching maturity attractive from time to time. Federally sponsored agencies such as the Federal Land Bank, the Federal Home Loan Bank, the Bank for Co-operatives, the Federal Intermediate Credit Bank, and the Federal National Mortgage Association are also empowered to issue securities to support their operations. The credit of such securities is high, even though there is no direct access to the Treasury for repayment, and their marketability is broad but not as good as that of Treasury bills. The somewhat lower quality of credit and marketability is reflected in the high yield afforded by these securities, which tends to be greater than that of Treasury securities with comparable maturities.

State and municipal securities. Because state and municipal obligations have the taxing power of the issuer behind them, high-quality issues supported by fiscally sound governments provide safe investments. The large number of tax exempt notes and bonds available enables an investor to choose maturities of one or two months, a year, or longer. However, for such obligations to be attractive to an investor, the corporation must be able to make use of the security's tax exemption privilege, and the complexities involved in interpreting the IRS code make it necessary to have competent legal and tax counsel before investing.

The marketability of state and municipal obligations

can vary widely, particularly when changes in the IRS code occur or large amounts of such obligations come to market; however, it is often possible to purchase securities to specific dates desired. Also, although most securities are purchased with federal funds, many state and municipal securities are settled in clearing house funds, which means a difference of one day in funds availability. Therefore, it is necessary to understand what funds are required for payment and in which form payment will be made at maturity, especially if the security matures on a Friday in clearing house funds. Another point to consider in the purchase of state and municipal securities is the place of payment. If payment is made in another part of the country, it will be necessary to pay insurance costs to ship the securities, and there may be a delay in transferring funds from the paying bank to the corporation's bank account.

Bank certificates of deposit. Since 1961, commercial banks have been issuing interest-bearing time certificates of deposit in negotiable form. These certificates were first developed by the large New York City banks to attract short-term corporate funds that were being invested in various short-term money market instruments. Essentially a device for paying interest on deposits or purchasing money, the certificates of deposit of large, well-known money-center banks quickly gained wide acceptance since the yields were competitive and marketability through the dealers' secondary markets was reasonably good. Currently, restrictions as to issuance and rate are included in Regulation Q of the Federal Reserve.

Bank holding company paper. Bank holding company paper is issued by a holding company whose principal asset is ownership of the stock of a bank. The device was used by commercial banks to attract funds when the ceiling on interest rates under Regulation Q made certificates of deposit noncompetitive, since the ceiling did not apply to this kind of investment. As a result, a bank could buy funds above the Regulation Q rates through the sale of holding company paper, which could then be advanced to the bank for its use. Such paper is not marketable but may be purchased for very short maturities at attractive rates.

Time deposits. Nonnegotiable time deposits, both foreign and domestic, are time deposits contracted to remain with a bank for a specific period of time. Such deposits may be made for banking as well as investment considerations where a bank relationship does not issue negotiable certificates of deposit.

Bankers acceptances. Bankers acceptances are time bills of exchange drawn on and accepted by a bank. Such drafts are used in both domestic and international finance, and they are self-liquidating. Since they arise only out of commercial transactions or dollar exchange, availability, dollar amounts, and the maturity limitation of 180 days may make it somewhat difficult to match the purchase of acceptances with a specific maturity or dollar amount required.

A broad market exists for the purchase and sale of acceptances, and at present several dealers make a market in acceptances. The quoted rates on acceptances normally do not fluctuate as freely as those on many other money market instruments, so there is somewhat less exposure to market risks.

Finance paper. Finance paper is sold by sales finance companies directly or through an investment banker to the investor. Although there is no secondary market for finance paper, repurchase by the issuer can be arranged—but the terms of repurchase should be thoroughly understood before a purchase is made. The quality of the paper can vary considerably, with the highest quality rated "prime." Such paper represents discounted, unsecured promissory notes of the issuer with maturities for as short as 1 or 2 days, or as long as 270 days. It is important to be able to raise the funds to retire maturing paper as it comes due, should the money market become unsettled, and to understand the relationship of the amount of outstanding paper to the available credit lines. The usual alternative source of funds to a paper-issuing company is its commercial banks. Many times the risk of solvency of a poorer credit is not warranted by the small disparity in rate.

Industrial paper. Unsecured promissory notes can be issued by industrial firms, with "prime" paper being issued by those companies with the best credit ratings. Industrial paper, unlike finance paper (which is generally self-liquidating), is issued to finance inventories and receivables, or to serve as a means of financing at a rate less than the corresponding bank lending rates. It is sold through dealers on a discount basis with maturities from 30 to 120 days. The financial strength of the issuer's ability to repay must be judged as well as the reputation of the dealer who is selling the paper, if the risk:return relationship is to be fully understood.

Foreign securities. Corporations with worldwide activities and interests may find it advantageous to invest in securities of other countries, notably those of Canada and the United Kingdom, when the combination of interest rates and hedge makes such investment attractive. Canadian commercial paper issued by the foreign finance subsidiaries of major U.S. corporations has been of particular interest when such paper is guaranteed by the parent U.S. corporation. Repurchase conditions of such paper before maturity must be understood by the purchaser, especially since these conditions are further complicated by the necessity of undoing the exchange agreement. Nonresident holders of Canadian commercial paper are subject to a 15 percent withholding tax at maturity.

Repurchase agreements. The simultaneous purchase and sale of a particular security at a specified yield have been proved useful for supplemental day-to-day investing of large sums. Such agreements allow the securities dealer to carry his inventory at a more reasonable cost, and they give an investor a good day-to-day return approximately in line with the funds rate, depending on the availability of securities for such purposes. The investor can be protected by arranging the purchase and sale at a sufficient discount should the sales agreement be broken. Such arrangements should be made only with those dealers in whom the investor has absolute confidence, because the return for the invested funds is not worth any risk of confidence.

Repurchase agreements are particularly helpful in periods when the day-to-day need for funds is unclear and market trends are not promising for securities of longer maturities. The quality of the repurchase agreement in such uncertain periods is controlled by the collateral used and the dealers' financial strength and integrity.

The Portfolio Mix

The portfolio mix of a short-term investment program will be governed primarily by management's philosophy concerning such assets and their intended use. Companies with small portfolios and limited availability of funds may invest only in Treasury bills, while corporations with a larger accumulation of resources may use many different money market instruments at the same time to maximize yield and retain adequate protection to meet the corporate objectives. For these corporations, the prime determinants of security mix in their portfolios are the trends in interest rates and liquidity in the money market. If the market is appraised correctly and corresponding adjustments are made as the market changes, the cash manager can improve the return on surplus cash and be assured of the liquidity of these assets in difficult times.

5

Appraising and Trading in the Money Market

H~EADLINES~ in the financial sections of newspapers and magazines propound various opinions on the future interest rates and the market outlook. The main difficulty in understanding the money market lies in sifting through the wealth of available statistical material to arrive at the factors that have the greatest influence on interest rates and the money market in general. Three basic areas must be considered in evaluating the money market: (1) the probable course of monetary policy as controlled by the Federal Reserve; (2) Treasury requirements for financing the operations of the federal government; and (3) the probable supply–demand relationships of available funds in the credit markets.

The Federal Reserve has been known to be somewhat secretive in discussing policy that will ease or restrict credit. Those involved in attempting to predict the level or direction of short-term interest rates are continually looking for clues concerning current Federal Reserve policy by analyzing the weekly Federal Reserve figures. Interpreting such published figures on a week-to-week basis is difficult at best, but because of the size of the money market and the potential rewards, there are many who follow these changes in an effort to gain some insight into the future trend in interest rates. Perhaps the most frequently used summation of the weekly figures is the position of the net free reserves of the commercial banking system. This figure represents the amount of funds available in the system in excess of the reserve requirements established by the Federal Reserve for bank deposits. When reserve requirements begin to exceed the funds free for lending and investment, money is less readily available in the banking system, and pressures for banks to regain liquidity through the sale of investments or purchase of funds soon begins to exert an upward pressure on money rates.

The federal funds rate—that is, the rate at which banks sell excess reserves to one another—usually gives a quick indication of the demands being exerted on the banking system to maintain liquidity, and as a result it is the most volatile rate. A relatively new measurement has been introduced in an attempt to understand the trends in monetary policy better by means of a periodic measurement of the money supply through its components—currency, demand, and time deposits—or by means of the aggregate bank credit proxy. The probable cause for this development is a feeling that the Federal Reserve, in making policy, has become more concerned with the rate of growth of the money supply in addition to its concern about the level of interest rates.

The activity of the Federal Reserve's Open Market Operations will at times give some indication of whether the

Federal Reserve is increasing or decreasing reserves and whether it is stabilizing security prices and easing dealer inventory problems, particularly during periods of monetary strain or during a Treasury financing. When the Federal Reserve is faced with accommodating several objectives that are in some respects conflicting, analysis of monetary trends becomes exceedingly difficult. This uncertainty is quickly reflected in the market as dealers begin to widen the spread between the bid and ask prices on money market instruments in an effort to protect themselves in the event that the market suddenly goes against them and prices deteriorate.

The fiscal operations of the Treasury, funding the costs of government, have a significant impact on the market and the level of interest rates. The amounts of new money to be raised to finance a cash deficit in government operations creates an added demand for funds that competes with the private sector of the economy. Treasury financing creates even greater pressures if fiscal requirements for cash develop at a time when monetary policy is limiting the growth in the money supply. Conversely, during periods when the money supply is expanding rapidly and there are relatively low demands for new government financing, the availability of funds in the private sector improves quickly, and, until demands for funds approach supply, interest rates will tend to decrease. This is a simplification of the problem, since different areas of the money market respond to change more rapidly than others (depending on the flow of funds within the money market itself), but a signal of a change in trend gives a good indication of changes within the market.

The cash budget of the Treasury indicates the peak periods of government demands for funds during its fiscal year. Typically, government financing requirements are heaviest during the first half of the fiscal year (July to December) and easiest in the second half (January to June). The cash requirements of the government combined with the seasonal needs of the private sector in the fourth quarter of the calendar year tend to put the greatest pressure on money market rates during this period, after which there is a noticeable easing of pressures in the first part of the new year as private seasonal demands subside and quarterly and final income tax payments are received by the Treasury.

The flow of funds through the credit markets is influenced by monetary policy through credit availability, fiscal demands from the Treasury, demands for funds from the private sector, and the rate of savings in the private sector. The total supply–demand relationships as expressed in this flow of funds gives a good insight into the possible trends in the level of interest rates.

To illustrate these supply–demand relationships, Exhibit 7 indicates the source and application of funds through the U.S. credit markets, along with the yield levels on various types of securities. The time deposit figures indicate the control of money supply through Regulation Q in 1966 and 1969, and are reflected in the contraction of total funds in these years as measured against the prior years. This reduction in funds resulted in a dramatic increase in all yield levels shown. The increase in deposits in 1967, which seemed to compensate more than adequately for the increase in government financing by the large increase in total available funds, enabled the credit markets to absorb easily the large amounts of government issues that came to the market. In 1969, when in fact government financing was declining from the previous year, this decline was more than offset by the drastic decline in the deposits component of money supply. The increases in funds were derived from the issuance of other credit instruments such as bank holding company paper and the attraction of foreign funds and funds from other sources that were attracted by the historically high interest rate levels of 1969.

Projections and estimates of the flow of funds through the credit markets enable the financial officer to get a

Exhibit 7

Source and Application of Funds in the U.S. Credit Markets
($ Billions)

	1965	1966	1967	1968	1969
Source of Funds					
Time deposits	32.7	19.7	39.1	33.1	−4.1
Demand deposits	8.0	4.0	11.6	11.2	5.5
Credit market inst.	5.6	19.1	−3.0	13.8	38.9
Foreign funds	.8	.7	5.0	4.0	10.4
U.S. government loans	2.8	4.9	4.6	5.2	2.6
Private ins. and pen. res.	15.7	16.7	18.7	18.2	18.7
Other sources	5.8	3.8	5.6	13.2	15.8
Total source of funds	71.4	68.9	81.6	98.7	87.8
Application of Funds					
U.S. government	1.7	3.5	13.0	13.4	−3.6
Foreign	2.6	1.5	4.1	3.0	3.5
State and local govt.	7.6	6.4	7.9	10.2	8.9
Households	28.8	23.2	19.7	31.8	31.4
Nonfinancial business	29.6	33.8	37.9	39.1	48.1
Net change in treas. bal.	1.1	.5	−1.0	1.2	−0.5
Total funds applied	71.4	68.9	81.6	98.7	87.8
Selected Yields Levels					
Federal funds	4.07	5.11	4.22	5.66	8.22
3-month bills	3.95	4.85	4.30	5.33	6.64
3–5 year	4.22	5.16	5.07	5.59	6.85
State and local AAA	3.16	3.67	3.74	4.20	5.45
Corporate AAA	4.49	5.13	5.51	6.18	7.03

Source: Federal Reserve Bulletin.

better perspective of what kind of overall money market conditions he may expect. A study of the trends in credit markets also assists him in developing a program concerning the long- and short-term financing requirements of the corporation and its demands for credit in the capital and money markets. If he concludes that conditions in the money market favor a relatively flat or declining trend in future money rates, he may wish to consider ways of improving the yield on money available for investment without impairing corporate objectives.

The Yield Curve

The basic concept for improving yield on a short-term portfolio without changing its characteristics is based on the fact that time is money and the future is uncertain. A security with a short maturity should yield less than a comparable security with a longer maturity in order to compensate for the increased market and/or credit risk until the principal is repaid.

Exhibit 8 indicates two yield curves on Treasury bills expressed in terms of the different yields on various maturities for two specific dates. The June 1, 1970, yield curve appears much steeper and reflects more concern about potential market risk than does the relatively more stable period reflected in the August 3, 1970, yield curve. However, if attitudes towards interest rates could be frozen for one year, yields in either case could be increased by buying long maturities, holding them for a period of time, and then selling them before maturity—as opposed to merely holding an original purchase until maturity.

The strategy in playing a yield curve is based on buying longer issues at higher yield levels and selling the security

Exhibit 8

**Yield Curve on Treasury Bills (bid)
on June 1, 1970, and August 3, 1970**

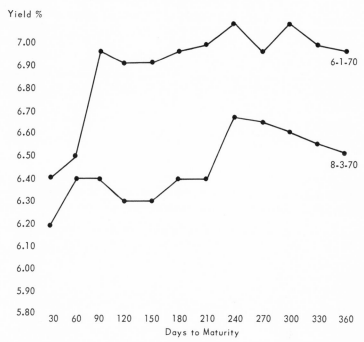

Source: First National City Bank Quotation Sheets, June 2, 1970, and August 4, 1970.

at lower levels. This can be done because the security is then closer to maturity, with some of the uncertainty of time removed. Another longer maturity can then be bought at a higher yield because the time-uncertainty factor has been increased. The timing of "trades" can be influenced by the shape of the current yield curve and the expectation of future yield curves.

Playing the yield curve is not an automatic guarantee

of higher returns, and in fact at times it may be impossible to increase yields; however, as long as the change in expectation of future interest rates is not greater than the differential between maturities, playing the yield curve should improve yields as opposed to buying and holding a security to maturity. A prime ingredient in playing such a curve is a broad, liquid, secondary market.

Playing the yield curve also encourages the readier adjustment of a portfolio to changing market conditions and overall corporate objectives and liquidity requirements. It serves as a constant reminder of the need for appraising the liquidity of the market.

Portfolios with a strong liquidity consideration tend to reduce market risk brought about by price fluctuation by limiting maturities to one year or less. Although the illustration in Exhibit 8 was concerned with Treasury bills, the same opportunities have been available with other short-term instruments such as certificates of deposit, tax-exempt notes, federal agencies, and bonds and notes that are nearing maturity.

"Rolling Over" and "Swapping"

A method commonly used in playing the yield curve is to participate in each week's auction of Treasury bills and then sell those bills to participate in the next week's auction. This method assumes that over a period of time the spread between the price of the new security and its sale price will be greater than any price decline that is caused by changing market conditions. A purchaser has the option of bidding for bills directly, bidding through a bank at his own price, or bidding with a bank. Each auction is different; sometimes the bidding is aggressive and at other times it is not. An indication of the aggressiveness of an auction is the variation between the average price bid for bills and the cheapest price paid for a winning bid. If there is little variation, it indicates that the bills sold very well and there should be a good aftermarket because many who may have wanted bills were unsuccessful in their bid. Conversely, unless the bid was on the low end of a wide variation, it is likely that the aftermarket for those bills will be such that it will be difficult if not impossible to improve the yield on the sale.

Rolling over bills for yield improvement is based on leverage. Appendix 4 indicates the dollar value of .01 percent discounted for each $1 million investment. An investment in six-month bills increases the return on the investment by $50 if the yield on that investment declines .01 percent. A quarter-point decline in the yield level will afford an additional $1,250 profit on the investment. If the investment had been made in 90-day bills, the increase of .01 percent in yield would be worth $25, and a quarter-point decline in yield would increase expected earnings by $625 for the period in which the security was held. The increase in maturity magnifies the potential profit or loss from a small change in yield levels.

Swapping improves the yield of securities similar in both quality and maturity by taking advantage of discrepancies that occur in the supply–demand balance of particular securities. There are occasions when two similar securities will trade out of line, causing a yield disparity with each other because of a sale of a new issue with a similar maturity or the appearance of a large secondary offering in the market. When this occurs, it is possible to improve the yield by selling a security that is not under any market pressure and buying the one that appears to be under pressure. Swapping attempts to improve yield by taking advantage of changes in the inventories of dealers and securities available in the market.

Trading for Tax Considerations

The most important income to a corporation is after-tax dollars. Before trading a portfolio, it is essential to understand the effect of corporate income and capital gains taxes on the corporation. The corporate tax manager can be helpful in suggesting the type of income that would be most beneficial to the corporation after tax considerations. For example, tax-exempt securities may look extremely attractive because of the after-tax yield based on current income tax rates. However, if a corporation's current borrowings jeopardize the ability to have such income allowed as tax-exempt under the IRS code, the after-tax return may be considerably lower than expected. In cases where tax-exempt securities can be used, further advantages are possible to the corporation that understands the exemption privileges available under state tax laws.

Capital gains tax rates, rather than income tax rates, apply on a portion of the income of certain securities that are purchased for less than their par value. The yield on securities that return income partially taxed on a capital gains basis can effectively increase the after-tax return above what a comparable, fully taxable security might yield. This differential in yield increases further if a corporation has established capital losses in other areas of operations and can use gains to offset losses. Such gains in a portfolio, in effect, would not be taxed at all. In trading securities that are selling below par it is important to be sure that the security can be held long enough to be taxed at capital gains rates, and that its maturity upon sale is sufficiently long to enable the buyer to take advantage of capital gains income at maturity.

Participating in New Issues

When the Treasury refunds maturing obligations, it usually offers the holders of the maturing issues the right to purchase the new issue. However, in order to insure the success of the refunding, the new issues are offered at rates higher than those currently prevailing in the market. Because the new securities are out of line with existing comparable securities, they have a tendency to seek the general market level for that type of security and trade at a premium. The fact that it is necessary to exchange the maturing security in order to purchase the new issue imputes a certain added value to the maturing security.

A trader tries to anticipate those refundings for which he expects there will be a rights offering and a heavy demand for the new security. He has the option of selling the old security with its "rights value" included in the price he receives, or he may accept the new security for the refunded issue and then sell it. The value of rights can fluctuate widely, depending upon the demand for the new security at the time of the announcement concerning the refunding and when the refunding is completed.

Alternatives to Trading

Although trading securities and anticipating turns in interest rate levels in the money market can be very advantageous in improving yield, there are times when market conditions do not warrant the exposure to market risk.

Yield and liquidity can be maintained best by using high-quality money market instruments with short maturities that insure quick repayment of both principal and interest without loss from the contracted rate and offer the opportunity to reinvest the funds at higher rates as the interest rate level rises. Unless an investor protects himself with the right maturity, not only can he lose the liquidity of short-term funds for corporate purposes but he can be locked into interest rates that may shortly be under the market.

Repurchase agreements on a day-to-day, weekly, or good-till-canceled basis offer good maturity protection for liquidity and rate in poor markets. Commercial paper, particularly finance company paper, is also available, as a rule, for short maturities of five to fourteen days. However, in poor markets when protection is needed most, quality is essential to insure against any complications that may arise during the repayment of principal or interest at maturity.

The final decision on the necessity to trade securities for the improvement of yield will depend on the types of securities available that meet corporate requirements and the yield differential between them. If two securities are available, one of which has a high yield and matures when cash will be required, and another of which has a lower yield but will require aggressive trading to raise the yield to a comparable level, there is little reason for assuming the trading risks to increase the yield. However, when yields of satisfactory instruments are relatively close and trading conditions appear attractive, trading should be pursued.

6

Measurement of
Portfolio Efficiency

THERE is a tendency to measure the performance
of a portfolio in absolute terms and to conclude that the
portfolio with the highest yield return has performed best.
Although a higher return on investments must be appre-
ciated, no comparison of results can be meaningful unless
performance is measured against the objectives of a portfolio. A corporate short-term portfolio with funds that are
available only for a short period of investment probably
will not have the same selection and flexibility of money
market instruments as will a portfolio whose funds will not
be required for corporate purposes for some time and are
therefore more readily available for investment.

The performance of a short-term portfolio should be
considered within the framework of the corporate objectives and management investment philosophy, and should
be evaluated on the basis of the selection of investments

available, the corporate fund requirements, the outlook for interest rates, the average maturity of the instruments used during the period evaluated, and the total average return on all investments held over a given period as compared with some standard measurement such as Treasury bill yields.

Interest Computation Methods

Yield measurement of a portfolio is complicated by the various ways in which interest may be calculated. The following are some of the methods used for interest computation on the more common money market instruments.

• Securities discounted on actual days to maturity on a 360-day year:

U.S. Treasury bills.

Bankers acceptances.

Bank holding company paper.

Commercial paper—

Sales finance.

Dealer finance.

Industrial.

• Securities discounted on actual days to maturity on a 365-day year:

United Kingdom Treasury bills.

Canadian Treasury bills.

Canadian commercial paper—

Sales finance.

• Securities discounted with each month having 30 days on a 360-day year:

Short-term tax-exempts.

• Interest-bearing securities with interest payable at maturity on actual days on a 360-day year:
  Negotiable certificates of deposit.
  Domestic commercial paper—
    Sales finance.
    Dealer finance.
    Industrial.
  Repurchase agreements.
  U.S. dollar deposits with Canadian banks.
  Eurodollar deposits.
• Interest-bearing securities with interest payable at maturity on actual days on a 365-day year:
  Canadian commercial paper—
    Sales finance.
    Industrial.
  U.S. dollar deposits at Canadian banks.
  United Kingdom hire purchase paper (sales finance).
  United Kingdom local authority paper (municipal).
• Interest-bearing securities with interest payable at maturity and each month having 30 days on a 360-day year:
  Tax-exempt notes.
• Interest-bearing securities with interest payable periodically on actual days on a 365-day year:
  Canadian dollar deposits.
• Interest-bearing securities with interest payable periodically and each month having 30 days on a 360-day year:
  Federal agency obligations.
  Tax-exempts—
    Notes.
    Bonds.
  Equipment trust certificates.
  Corporate bonds.
• Interest-bearing securities with interest payable periodi-

cally on the basis of the actual days in the coupon period, which may vary from 181 to 184 days:

U.S. Treasury—
Notes.
Bonds.
Certificates of indebtedness.

If there is to be a meaningful measurement, some common basis for comparison must be established. The most common basis for quoting yields is an annualized bond equivalent yield basis. Measurement of yield is further complicated by the difference between yields before and after tax. An adjustment is necessary to place income that is tax-exempt or subject to capital gains rates on the same basis as ordinary income.

Measuring Yield Comparability

Yield comparability is essential in evaluating alternative instruments at the time of purchase. Many of the money market instruments that are sold on a discount basis are also quoted on a bond equivalent yield basis in many dealers' quotation sheets. The formula used by the Treasury on short bills is

$$i = \left(\frac{100}{P} - 1 \right) \frac{365}{N}$$

where i = coupon issue equivalent
yield (interest)
N = actual number of days
P = price

Example: $1,000,000 Treasury bill purchased on June 3, 1970, maturing September 3, 1970, at a discount of 6.85%.

Discount for 92 days @ 6.85% on $1,000,000 = $17,505.56

$1,000,000 − $17,505.56 = $982,494.44 or $98.249 per $100

$$i = \left(\frac{100}{98.249} - 1 \right) \frac{365}{92}$$

$$.017822 \times \frac{365}{92} = 7.07 \text{ Bond Equivalent Yield}$$

The same type of conversion of discount yield to bond equivalent yield would apply to discounted commercial paper. Conversion of yield on interest-bearing securities as CDs or time deposits (360) at par would be

$$\frac{365 \times i}{360}$$

In the case of securities with interest computed on the basis of a 30-day month in a 360-day year, it is necessary to adjust expected yield on a short maturity to an annualized bond equivalent yield, in order to account for the difference between the days in which interest is earned on a 30-day month and the actual days involved. The formula for this is

$$\frac{\text{yield} \times \text{days interest is earned} \div 360}{\text{actual days}} \times 365$$

Tax-exempt yield and income subject to capital gains are adjusted to reflect the after-tax advantage.

Conversion of interest rates to a common basis. Exhibit 9 illustrates the conversion of the yields on discounted securities to an annualized bond equivalent basis by use of the formula given earlier for Treasury bills. Many discount tables provide the comparable bond equivalent yield along with the discount price for convenience. The yields on the tax-exempt and the FICBs are adjusted for securities with interest on a 30- to 360-day basis, and the yield on the tax-exempt is doubled to reflect the 50 percent rate assumed.

Exhibit 9

Conversion of Interest Rates to a Common Basis
Annualized Bond Equivalent Yield

	Face Amount	Principal Cost	Purchase Yield	Purchase Date	Maturity	Actual Days to Maturity	Earning Days to Maturity	Annual-ized Bond Equiva-lent Yield
U.S. Treasury bills	$1,000,000	$ 982,494.44	6.85%	6– 3–70	9– 3–70	92	92	7.07
Commercial paper	1,000,000	986,444.44	8.00	6– 3–70	8– 3–70	61	61	8.22
Tax-exempts	1,000,000	1,000,000.00	5.75	6–15–70	12–15–70	183	180	11.46*
FICBs**	1,000,000	1,000,000.00	8.15	6– 1–70	3– 1–71	273	270	8.17
Total	$4,000,000	$3,968,938.88						

* 50% tax rate.
** Federal intermediate credit bank notes.

Computation of average maturities. Exhibit 10 shows a method of measuring the average maturity. This average is arrived at by multiplying the principal cost of each investment (column 1) by the number of days to maturity (column 2) to find the number of investment days to maturity for each security (column 3). The total investment days for each security (column 3) divided by the total principal cost of investments (column 1) equals the average maturity of the short-term portfolio.

Exhibit 10

Computation of Average Maturities

	(1)	(2)	(3)
	Principal Cost $\times$	Actual Days to Maturity =	Investment Days
U.S. Treasury bills	$ 982,494.44	92	90,573,488
Commercial paper	986,444.44	61	60,173,111
Tax-exempts	1,000,000.00	183	183,000,000
FICBs	1,000,000.00	273	273,000,000
	$3,968,938.88		606,746,599

$$\text{Average maturity} = \frac{606,746,599}{3,968,938} = 153 \text{ days}$$

Computation of average investment and average yield for June 1970. Exhibit 11 shows the derivation of two important figures that are significant in preparing monthly reports to management concerning the results of the portfolio. Average investment is developed by multiplying the principal cost (column 1) of each security by the number of days it is held during a measurement period (column 2) in order to arrive at investment days in the period (column 3). The average investment then equals the total investment days accumulated in the period (June) divided by the number of days in the period (30 days).

Exhibit 11

Computation of Average Investment and Average Yield for June 1970

	(1) Principal Cost	(2) Days Investment Held in Period*	(3) Investment Days	(4) Annualized Bond Equivalent Yield	(5) Yield Weighted Investment Days
U.S. Treasury bills	$ 982,494.44	28	27,509,844	7.07	1,944,946
Commercial paper	986,444.44	28	27,620,444	8.22	2,270,400
Tax-exempts	1,000,000.00	16	16,000,000	11.46	1,833,600
FICBs	1,000,000.00	30	30,000,000	8.17	2,451,000
	$3,968,938.88		101,130,288		8,499,946

* Interest begins on date of purchase.

$$\text{Average investment} = \frac{\text{investment days}}{\text{days in the month}} = \frac{101,130,288}{30} = 3,371,009$$

$$\text{Average yield} = \frac{\text{yield weighted}}{\text{investment days}} = \frac{8,499,946}{101,130,288} = 8.406\%$$

$$\text{Approx. accrued income for month} = \frac{3,371,009 \times 8.406\% \times 30}{365} = 23,294$$

The average yield for the period is found by multiplying the investment days (column 3) by the bond equivalent yield of each investment held (column 4) to arrive at the yield weighted investment days (column 5). The total of the yield weighted investment days (column 5) divided by the total investment days (column 3) equals the average annualized bond equivalent yield on all investments during the period being measured.

The interest accrual for the month, adjusted for tax-exempt income, should equal $23,294, which in turn should equal the total of the monthly accounting accrual for interest earned on investments adjusted to reflect the tax-exempt income for June:

$$\$3,371,009 \times 8.406\% \times \frac{30}{365} = \$23,294 \text{ accrued income}$$

Therefore, if the accrued income is known from accounting accruals, and the average daily investment is known, the annualized bond equivalent yield may be found by the method shown in Exhibit 12.

Standard Measurements and Reports

The development of a standard to measure performance can probably be best expressed in a range whose minimum is considered to be the yield on Treasury bills equal to the portfolio's average maturity. Good performance can be equated with the yield expected on a mix of investments that satisfy corporate objectives and management philosophy. Excellent performance would exceed the yield expected on a proper mix of investments if trading techniques were used, and would avoid jeopardizing corporate objectives or exceeding the authority outlined by the management policy or philosophy.

Exhibit 12

Accounting Accruals

Purchase Rate		Principal Cost	Actual Days to Maturity	Est. Earnings to Maturity	Est. Daily Accrual	Days Investment Held in Period	Accrued Earnings for Period	Adjustment for Tax Exemption and Capital Gains
6.85	U.S. Treasury bills	$ 982,494.44	92	$17,505.56	$190.28	28	$ 5,327.79	
8.00	Commercial paper	986,444.44	61	13,555.56	222.22	28	6,222.22	
5.75	Tax-exempts	1,000,000.00	183	28,750.00	157.10	16	2,513.66	$2,513.66
8.15	FICBs	1,000,000.00	273	61,125.00	223.90	30	6,717.03	
		$3,968,938.88					$20,780.69	

Total Average Earnings $23,294

A monthly report indicating the month-end mix of investments, bond equivalent yields, and maturity range gives a good indication to management of the liquidity and return being earned on the portfolio at any given time. A report should also include some appraisal of the money market and the direction in which the portfolio mix and maturities should move in order to remain consistent with corporate objectives. The inclusion of average investment, accrued income, and yield over a given period provides management with a quick appraisal of past results, and a total listing of securities held at the end of the reporting period allows management to review the individual securities held and the amounts involved in each investment. Such disclosure on a periodic basis will enable the the portfolio manager and management to understand more fully the problems of corporate financing and the money and credit markets.

A Final Word

Money, like any other raw material or commodity has a cost, and over the past 25 years that cost has been steadily increasing. In attempting to reduce costs and improve their operations, more and more corporations have come to realize the importance of good cash management, particularly since the competition for funds has been so keen at times that some would-be borrowers have been denied access to the funds that they need for the continued growth of their corporations.

The combined problems of cost and availability of funds have created a greater need for improving methods to establish the amount of money required to operate a corporation successfully. In addition, the corporation must analyze its cash operations to be sure that control and safekeeping of funds are secure and that the corporation is getting the maximum availability and use of the funds at its disposal.

Appendixes

Appendix 1

Interest Earned per Day (365-Day Basis) on $1,000,000
(*See Chapter 4*)

Coupon Rate (percent)	Daily Interest per $1,000,000
1 1/2	$ 41.10
2 1/2	68.49
3 1/4	90.28
3 1/2	95.89
4	109.59
4 1/4	116.44
4 3/4	130.14
5	136.99
5 1/4	143.84
5 3/4	157.53
6	164.38
6 1/2	178.08
7	191.78
7 1/2	205.48
8	219.18
8 1/2	232.88

Appendix 2

Common Money Market Instruments
(*See Chapter 4*)

	Obligation	*Market-ability*	*Maturities*	*Minimum Denomi-nations ($)*
U.S. Treasury bills	U.S. Treasury obligation	Excellent	Up to 1 year	10,000
U.S. Treasury notes, bonds	U.S. Treasury obligation	Very good	1 year and longer	1,000
U.S. agency notes, debs., and bonds	Authorized by U.S. Congress	Very good	6 months and longer	5,000
Negotiable time certs. of deposit	Certs. of a time dep. at comm. bank	Good	30 days and longer	100,000–500,000
Bank holding co. paper	Promissory note of a bank holding company	No market-ability; will buy back subject to rate adjustment	Any date 5 days and longer	100,000
Sales finance paper	Promissory note of finance co. directly placed with investor	No market-ability; will usually buy back subject to rate adjustment	Any date 3 days to 270 days	100,000 25,000 on 30 day and longer maturities
Dealer paper finance	Promissory note of finance co. sold through dealers	No market-ability; buy back can usually be arranged through a dealer	Issued for any date from 30 to 270 days	100,000–500,000

	Obligation	*Market-ability*	*Maturities*	*Minimum Denominations ($)*
Dealer paper industrial	Promissory notes of inds. firms sold through dealer	No market-ability; arrangement can be made for repurchase through a dealer	Issued for specific dates, 30 to 180 days	100,000–500,000
Prime bankers acceptances	Time draft accepted by a bank	Good	Up to 1 year	1,000
Short-term tax-exempts (public house)	Local notes secured by fed. agencies contract and U.S. Treas.	Good	Up to 1 year	1,000
Short-term tax-exempts (state and local)	Notes of state municipalities and political subdivisions	Fairly marketable	Up to 1 year	1,000
Repurchase agreement	Any security desired or available	None	One day and longer	500

Appendix 3

Computation of Principal Protection
on Treasury Bills from Market Changes
(*See Chapter 4*)

I. The number of days a bill must be held to avoid principal loss from a decline in yield after purchase is computed as—

$$Dms = \frac{Dmp \times ip}{is}$$

where: Dms = days to maturity at date of sale
Dmp = days to maturity at day of purchase
ip   = purchase yield
is   = sale yield

Example: For a 90-day bill purchased to yield 6.50% and sold to yield 6.75%, the length of time to be held to avoid principal loss is—

$$\frac{90 \times 6.50}{6.75} = 86.67$$

Days to maturity at date of purchase	90
Days to maturity at date of sale	86
Days security must be held to avoid principal loss	4

II. The yield at which a bill can be sold without loss of principal after 14 days is computed as—

$$is = \frac{Dmp \times ip}{Dms}$$

Example: For a 90-day bill purchased to yield 6.50% and sold after 14 days, the maximum yield at which it can be sold to avoid principal loss is—

$$is = \frac{90 \times 6.50}{76}$$

The sale yield may rise to 7.70 and still not cause a principal loss if the security is held 14 days. This can be proved by using the first formula:

$$76 = \frac{90 \times 6.50}{7.70}$$

Days to maturity at date of purchase	90
Days to maturity at date of sale	76
Days security must be held to avoid principal loss	14

Appendix 4

Dollar Value of .01% Discounted for Every $1,000,000
(*See Chapter 5*)

Days to Maturity	Dollar Value of .01%
1	.28
10	2.78
30	8.33
60	16.67
90	25.00
120	33.33
150	41.67
180	50.00
210	58.33
240	66.67
270	75.00
300	83.33
330	91.67
360	100.00

About the Author

Roger W. Hill, Jr. has been affiliated with National Distillers and Chemical Corporation since 1959, where he has been a member of the cash budgeting department, assistant cashier in cash management and short-term investments, and assistant treasurer in charge of investments. Previously, he was loan administrator and credit analyst for New York Trust Company, now a part of Chemical Bank. Mr. Hill obtained his A.B. in economics from the College of William and Mary in 1955, and his M.B.A. in investment from New York University in 1959.